TAKING A CANDID LOOK AT YOUR BUSINESS

Written by Jean Peterson
and Joel Virtue

Design and Layout by

authorHOUSE®

AuthorHouse™
1663 Liberty Drive
Bloomington, IN 47403
www.authorhouse.com
Phone: 833-262-8899

Published by AuthorHouse 07/05/2021

ISBN: 978-1-4184-8083-7 (sc)
ISBN: 978-1-4685-1990-7 (e)

Library of Congress Control Number: 2004097035

Print information available on the last page.

*Any people depicted in stock imagery provided by Getty Images are models,
and such images are being used for illustrative purposes only.
Certain stock imagery © Getty Images.*

This book is printed on acid-free paper.

Contents

Naked Business

Taking a Candid Look at Your Small Business

Con artists are everywhere. In fact, you look at one in the mirror each morning. It's true. We like to cover things up. And we're good at it. Whether it's the extra couple of pounds we've put on or the nagging debt that we've accumulated, we are masters of camouflage when it comes to handling issues with which we would rather not deal.

Face it. Few of us look forward to standing naked in front of the mirror. That's because the stark reality of our imperfections, yes, and those extra pounds, reflects loudly back at us. There's no covering the truth when you're in front of the mirror naked. There is only you and what you want to do about what you see – whether you like it or not.

Naked Business is about stripping away the camouflage around issues in your business. It's about taking a candid look at yourself, your company, and where you are versus where you want to be. Naked Business poses questions that only you can answer about yourself and your company.

We challenge you to answer each question honestly and in depth - to stand in front of the mirror naked, if you will. What you see as you answer these questions may terrify, surprise, or inspire you. Either way, you will have faced yourself and your problems. Then you can decide what you want to do with what you see. Best of luck!

NOW, LET'S GET NAKED

What About Me?

So, you started a small business. Congratulations! We're sure there were a lot of reasons why. Maybe you thought you'd make more money, have the freedom to set your own schedule, or enjoy being your own boss. Then, reality set in and you began to deal with common small business issues that no one told you about when you decided to go out on your own. Cash flow, time management, customer service, retention, balance sheets, profit and loss statements, office support, cold calls, sales, marketing and advertising - all vie for your attention and suddenly, you don't feel so good.

Owning and operating a small business can be one of the most challenging lessons in personal growth you've ever tackled. A savvy business owner needs to know him or herself like no one else does. That means undertaking an honest self-evaluation and dealing with the good, the bad, and the ugly. It's not easy, but by getting to know yourself personally, and as a business owner, you will save yourself time and money in the long run. Take a good look.

LET'S GET NAKED

What are your strengths and weaknesses? List them.
My strengths are...

_____

_____

_____

_____

_____

_____

My weaknesses are...

_____

_____

_____

_____

_____

_____

Ask others what your strengths and weaknesses are.

_____   _____

_____   _____

_____   _____

_____   _____

_____   _____

Are you a starter or a finisher? How do you know? _____

_____

_____

_____

_____

Why are you in business? What did you hope to achieve by starting your company? More money? More family time? Etc. _____

_____

_____

_____

_____

If you opened your business to have more family time, would your family agree that this is happening? Have you asked them what they think of the business? Ask them. Then listen with an open mind.

_____

_____

_____

_____

_____

_____

How do you handle failure? _____

_____

_____

_____

> *If you don't like to fail, you probably shouldn't be in business for yourself, because you will make mistakes. If you can make a mistake, learn from it and move on, go for it! If not, being in business for yourself may not be the way to go.*

Describe your personality. Are you flexible and able to roll with the punches or are you a by the book, ducks-in-a-row person? How will your personality be beneficial to your business? _____

_____

_____

_____

_____

_____

> *Most successful small business people know how to roll with the punches. You can be a "ducks-in-a-row-person" running a small business, just don't blow a gasket when things don't line up like you think they should. There are rebel ducks out there flying in forms over which you have no control. So, when unhappy customers, delayed shipments, poor employees, equipment malfunctions, or late payments come flying at you in a "Z", have a plan of action that will allow you to handle the situation.*

Are you a self-starter? Can you work alone? What do you do when you are alone? Describe your work habits. _____

_____

_____

_____

_____

_____

_____

> *If you are not able to pull yourself out of bed and work alone, turn around and go back to your 9 to 5. Many small business owners face the temptation to do the laundry, turn on the TV, or do any one of a million nagging little projects, especially if they work from home. However, if you are serious about succeeding in your own business, you need to be strong enough to hold yourself accountable for what you want to achieve.*

What do you want to achieve? How is it going to happen?

_____

_____

_____

_____

_____

_____

> *Like it or not, going into business is personal. Being in business is personal. Surviving in business is personal. Small business owners need to be able to operate in a variety of skill sets, be willing to take risks, and learn a little about a lot of things.*

What do you value most? i.e. time, freedom, money, recognition, etc. Why? _____

_____

_____

_____

What do you love to do? _____

_____

_____

_____

_____

_____

What do you dread doing? Who can do this for you? What will it take
to get to the point where you can hire this done? _____

_____

_____

_____

_____

_____

_____

> *Small business owners are notorious for doing everything themselves.
> While this may be necessary when you first start, set a goal to move
> toward hiring things done that either you're not good at doing, or that
> you would rather not do. You may have to swallow hard when you hire
> that first person, but if you stick to doing what you do best, your
> company will be more profitable in the long run.*

What types of people will you need in your organization in order for your business to grow? How will you use their skills? The challenge here is to surround yourself with people who are *not* like you. Strive to create balance in your company and leverage other people's strengths. _____

_____

_____

_____

_____

_____

_____

_____

What is your definition of success? How will you know when you've "made it"? _____

_____

_____

_____

_____

_____

_____

List the areas in which you feel least comfortable in regards to operating your business. Are you willing to admit what you don't know and get help in those areas? _____

_____

_____

_____

_____

What resources are recommended by successful business owners in your area? _____

_____

_____

_____

_____

> *Getting help can be a lot less expensive than going it on your own. There are valuable sources that offer free information for small business owners. (SBA – Small Business Administration, SCORE – Service Core of Retired Executives, Libraries, etc.) Just remember, some free advice may actually cost you down the road. Be careful where you get your information.*

Naked Business Reality: No one's going to take care of you but you. Learn to balance your time. Your business can and will eat every waking moment, if you don't set boundaries. Study the lives of successful people. Most of them commit themselves to down time - time to refresh and rejuvenate so they can give their best to their families and their business. Don't work yourself into the ground. Give yourself at least one day off per week.

What About My Company?

Small business owners have a tendency to jump into business and paddle happily along before they establish measurable goals and benchmarks for their new endeavor. They may be making money, but many times they are rowing with one oar instead of shooting the rapids like they originally intended. If you don't know where you want to go, how will you know when you get there?

LET'S GET NAKED

Do you have a mission/purpose statement for your company? What is it? Are you living up to that mission/purpose? _____

_____

_____

_____

Does your mission/purpose statement need to be revamped? If you've been in business for a while, you may find that your original purpose has changed. What is it now? _____

_____

_____

_____

If *you don't have a mission statement, we challenge you to create one. Your mission statement should serve as a guidepost for your company. It should be able to be clearly stated in no more than two sentences. You should state what it is you want to accomplish and how you want to accomplish it. A great resource for writing a mission statement is Ken Blanchard's book, "Full Steam Ahead".*

Do you have a balanced advisory board? Who would you like to have on your board? How can you create one? _____

_____

_____

_____

_____

_____

_____

Being in business for yourself is a strange combination of idealism and realism. Your job is to find the right mix of optimism and factual information that allows you to move forward and make plans during the tough times. Your position as a small business owner requires fortitude, creativity, ingenuity, and resourcefulness. You also need to be able to withstand pressure. If you thought working for another company was stressful, wait until a couple of clients are late with payment and you need to make payroll!

How can you continue your education and stay abreast of business developments in your industry and in your region? _____

_____

_____

_____

_____

Do you have a business plan? What do you find most challenging about your business plan? How will you overcome that challenge?

_____

_____

_____

_____

_____

_____

A business plan is a road map to help you grow your company. Check back with your plan periodically to make sure you are on the right track. If you don't have a business plan, you are stumbling around in the dark. Create one, however simple, to give you some guidelines so you aren't just flailing around in never-land.

Do you have a marketing plan? What do you find most challenging about your marketing plan? How will you overcome that challenge?

_____

_____

_____

_____

_____

> *Combining a great business plan with a great marketing plan is the key to success in business. Sadly, marketing is often the first thing that small companies put on the back burner when they get busy with the business of doing business. You should be thinking of marketing as dressing your business up and taking it to a party to meet potential clients.*

Is what you were hoping to achieve with your business happening? Why? Why not? What needs to change to make it happen?

_____

_____

_____

_____

_____

_____

Are you willing to set deadlines for achieving your goals? Jack Canfield and Mark Victor Hanson in "*The Power of Focus*" tell us that goals must be specific and measurable. List goals you have for your business. Now, list the time frames in which you hope to accomplish them.

_____   _____

_____   _____

_____   _____

_____   _____

> *Set some realistic goals. (Notice I said realistic, not engraved in stone.) If you aren't sure what's realistic, call on some outside advisors. There are many resources for small businesses out there.*

Now that you've determined your goals and deadlines, what are you going to do if they don't work? What are you going to do if they do work? _____

_____

_____

_____

_____

_____

_____

_____

What is your exit strategy? Do you know when you want to be done with your business and enjoying the good life? Write down your exit strategy and goals now. Remember to assign timelines.

_____

_____

_____

_____

_____

What About the Money?

Most likely, you started your business to make money. Great! The question is, are you comfortable handling money in the way it will need to be handled in a business setting? Financial statements are important. Learn how to read them and how to gauge how well your business is doing. If you have personal money issues deal with them now, before you get too far into business. How you handle your money in your personal life will be reflected in what you do with your company's funds.

LET'S GET NAKED

Make wise expenditures by asking yourself these three questions:

- Can I afford this?

- How can I afford this?

- Can I afford not to do/have this?

Could you make more working for someone else? If you can make more working for someone else, is that what you want to do? Why? Why not? _____

_____

_____

_____

_____

_____

How does money make you feel? What do you think about when you think of money? _____

_____

_____

_____

Are you under or overbidding? Why? _____

_____

_____

_____

_____

_____

_____

_____

Small business owners often underbid projects simply to get business in the door. While that might work short term, take a realistic look at the cost factor of doing so. Is it worth it when you calculate expenses including your time? It's tough to sell yourself as a small business. Yet if you have a great product or service and know your clients are getting what they're paying for, then set a fair price and stick to it.

Where can you find money for your business? Can you make the money you need with your business? How? _____

_____

_____

_____

_____

_____

_____

Have you determined a dollar amount for your initial investment into the company? Now, carefully list all expenses and possible expenses. Is your initial dollar amount sufficient to cover the next 6 months worth of expenses? _____

_____

_____

_____

_____

_____

_____

_____

What do you want your annual gross revenue to be? What do you want your annual gross profit to be? Is this enough to allow you the lifestyle you envision? _____

_____

_____

_____

_____

_____

Do you know where your money is coming from? Which clients are most profitable and why? List the clients with whom you enjoy working and see how much profit they add to your bottom line. Concentrate on those types of clients. _____

_____

_____

_____

_____

_____

Tracking where the majority of your profit is coming from would seem to be common sense. Yet, many small businesses don't adequately break down their income so that they can make the necessary adjustments to achieve the greatest bottom line.

What are your customers saying? Do you regularly get feedback from them? If not, how can you get feedback and leverage that information? _____

_____

_____

_____

_____

_____

Is e-commerce a component of your business that you should consider? Why or why not? _____

_____

_____

_____

_____

_____

_____

_____

What are you going to do regarding collections processes? Write out your strategy. _____

_____

_____

_____

_____

_____

_____

> Sad to say, but there are people in the world who will not pay on time. This is death to the small business owner who is operating on a shoe string budget. Establish collection procedures before you actually have a problem. If you can't bring yourself to make the calls, get someone who can, or hire a professional collection agency. Remember, this is business, and any other business wouldn't think twice about following up with you.

Are you going to or can you accept credit cards? There are a lot of options out there...it may be worth your time to research various card services to find the best option for you. Make a list of your options.

_____

_____

_____

_____

_____

Do you have "toxic" clients that are costing you time and/or money? How can you get rid of them? _____

_____

_____

_____

_____

_____

> *One of the hardest things about being in business for yourself is learning to let go of those clients who are costing you time and/or money. High maintenance clients may not be worth it, even if there is a fat paycheck dangling at the end of the stick. Establish parameters regarding client relations. If you need to "fire" a client, you can always refer them to your competition!*

How can you leverage technology? How can you make technology pay for itself? _____

_____

_____

_____

What About People?

The great thing about being in business for yourself is the people. The bad thing about being in business for yourself is the people. People are the magic ingredient in business and in life. But, there are a few people out there who seem to blow up the whole concoction. Your interpersonal relation skills will be invaluable as a business owner. From your best client to your most frustrating employee, you need to be able to relate to people in various capacities. If you are willing to learn, you don't have to be a "people person" in order to succeed. If you absolutely can't handle people, make sure someone in your organization can. People are what make your business work.

LET'S GET NAKED

What do you do best when it comes to dealing with people? _____

_____

_____

_____

_____

What do you need to improve in your interpersonal skills? _____

_____

_____

_____

Where can you learn or develop the people skills you are lacking?

_____

_____

_____

_____

_____

What is the most difficult interpersonal communication for you as relates to your business? What types of interpersonal communications come easily for you? Why? _____

_____

_____

_____

_____

_____

What do you like most about relating to people? _____

_____

_____

_____

What do you like least about relating to people? _____

_____

_____

_____

_____

_____

If you simply cannot stand people, who can you designate as the "people-handler" in your organization? Write a job description/ personality description for this person _____

_____

_____

_____

_____

How do you think people see you? Be descriptive. _____

_____

_____

_____

_____

Ask 3 other people how they see you professionally and personally.
Ask them to provide a descriptive paragraph about you.

1) _____

_____

_____

_____

_____

2) _____

_____

_____

_____

_____

3) _____

_____

_____

_____

What kinds of people do you enjoy most? _____

_____

_____

_____

_____

_____

What is your ideal client profile?   Not just financially, but
personality-wise. _____

_____

_____

_____

_____

_____

_____

Where can you find these ideal clients? _____

_____

_____

What do you think your ideal client thinks his ideal vendor would be like? _____

_____

_____

_____

_____

_____

_____

_____

Ask your ideal client what he is looking for in a vendor. _____

_____

_____

_____

As a business owner, do you have a support system in place? (Not just friends and family, but other business owners or professionals that you might be able to bounce ideas off.) How can you build a support system? _____

_____

_____

_____

_____

_____

> In just about any business success book, you will find that "the great ones" i.e. Carnegie, James J. Hill, Napoleon Hill, Henry Ford, etc. all say that you should surround yourself with experts or people who are more knowledgeable than you are, so you can leverage their abilities and focus on what you do best. Let's take their advice, and check it out! It obviously worked for them!

Do you have a business mentor? Where can you find one?

_____

_____

_____

_____

Write out 5 questions you would like to ask your mentor.

_____

_____

_____

_____

What About Sales?

Yes, we said it, the "S" word! Like it or not, as a small business owner, you do not have the luxury of saying you're not a sales person. By default, you have to be. That is a fact! You can hire a sales force, but no one will be as passionate about your company and your product as you are.

Whether you offer a product or service, sales are vital to the success of your company. No sales means no revenue. You simply cannot afford to ignore sales if you intend to succeed in business.

LET'S GET NAKED

What is your definition of sales? _____

_____

_____

_____

_____

_____

_____

What images does the word sales conjure up for you? _____

_____

_____

_____

_____

_____

_____

Where can you go to get sales training and information? Make a list of resources. _____

_____

_____

_____

_____

_____

What will obtaining training and information do for you and your company? _____

_____

_____

_____

_____

As a small business owner you wear many hats. While you don't have to be an expert in everything, a general working knowledge of the various functions within your company can be very helpful when making decisions. If you know the basics of selling, you'll be a more effective leader when it comes time to motivate your sales force, because you've been on the front lines.

Map out your sales cycle. How long does a normal sale take? Use this in your budgeting forecasts. _____

_____

_____

_____

_____

_____

_____

What would you like your sales cycle to look like? How can you make this happen? _____

_____

_____

_____

_____

Do you have an incentive system in place for your sales force? If so, is it working? What types of incentives could you offer?

_____

_____

_____

_____

_____

_____

Incentives don't have to cost money. Employees may want more family time, more free time, or more flexible hours. Find out what motivates the people working for you before you create your incentive program.

Do you have a sales manual? If not, create one, or have one created for your organization. It will save time and money in the long run. List some topics you would like to include in your manual.

_____

_____

_____

_____

_____

Do you have a job description for your sales force? Again, create one if you don't already have something in place. List your expectations. _____

_____

_____

_____

_____

_____

_____

_____

Do you have a "person" description for the type of person you want representing your company as a sales person? Write that description down so that when that person walks in the door, you will know it in an instant. Be thoughtful and creative in the attributes you list. _____

_____

_____

_____

_____

_____

Congratulations!

You've taken the first step toward doing Naked Business - taking a candid look and asking the difficult questions. More importantly, we hope you have answered some of these questions with answers that will help you get more out of your business. Remember, Naked Business is about revealing the truth, even if it's not what you were hoping to see. It's like standing in front of a mirror ~ you may not like what you see, but you have a choice as to what you do with it.

Naked Business is not meant to be a comprehensive business guide. Rather, it's meant to help you ask the questions that many small business owners tend to avoid. When you've been in front of the mirror once, it gets easier. Continue to practice Naked Business and you will benefit from it!

Feel free to contact us with questions, comments, or observations at Bright Ideas Group (a division of VP, Etc, Inc.), 5115 Excelsior Blv, Suite 338, Minneapolis, MN 55416, 612-290-6222, info@reallybrightideas.com.

Layout by Alia Design, www.alia-design.com, 651-503-7155

Bibliography

The Power of Focus
by Jack Canfield, Mark Victor Hansen, & Les Hewitt.
Deerfield Beach: Health Communications, 2000

Full Steam Ahead – Unleash the Power of Vision in Your Company and Your Life. by Ken Blanchard
Berret-Koehler Publishers, Inc.   San Francisco, CA 2003

Printed in the United States
by Baker & Taylor Publisher Services